DATE DUE

Bilingual Edition

READING POWER

Edición Bilingüe

Mia Hamm

Soccer Superstar

Superestrella del fútbol soccer

Heather Feldman

Traducción al español
Mauricio Velázquez de León

The Rosen Publishing Group's

PowerKids Press™ & **Buenas Letras**™
New York

1

For Sophie Megan
Para Sophie Megan

Published in 2002 by The Rosen Publishing Group, Inc.
29 East 21st Street, New York, NY 10010

First Bilingual Edition 2002
First Edition in English 2001

Book Design: Michael de Guzman

Photo Credits: p. 5 © Al Bello/ALLSPORT; p. 7 © Jamie Squire/ALLSPORT; pp. 9, 17 © Rob Tringali Jr./SportsChrome USA; p. 11 © Office of Sports Information, University of North Carolina; p. 13 © Mike Cooper/ALLSPORT; p. 15 © Andy Lyons/ALLSPORT; p. 19 © Brian Bahr/ALLSPORT; p. 21 © Vincent Laforet/ALLSPORT.

Feldman, Heather.
    Mia Hamm : soccer superstar = Mia Hamm : superestrella del fútbol soccer/ Heather Feldman : traducción al español Mauricio Velázquez de León.
        p. cm.— (Reading power)
    Includes bibliographical references and index.
    Summary: This book introduces Mia Hamm, one of the top female soccer players in the world.
    ISBN 0-8239-6136-2
    1. Hamm, Mia, 1972- —Juvenile literature. 2. Soccer players—United States— Biography—Juvenile literature. 3. Women soccer players—United States— Biography—Juvenile literature. [1. Hamm, Mia, 1972- 2. Soccer Players. 3. Women—Biography. 4. Spanish language materials—Bilingual.] I. Title. II. Series.

796.334'092—dc21
[B]

Word Count:
English: 173
Spanish: 197

Manufactured in the United States of America

Contents ━━━━━

━━━━━ Contenido

Mia Hamm plays soccer. Mia is a great soccer player.

———

Mia Hamm juega fútbol soccer. Mia es una gran jugadora de fútbol.

Mia kicks the soccer ball hard. She kicks the soccer ball into the goal net. Mia scores a goal.

———

Mia patea muy fuerte el balón. Cuando el balón entra en la portería, Mia anota un gol.

Mia can jump high.
She jumps up to get
the soccer ball.

———

Mia puede saltar muy
alto. Brinca para
alcanzar el balón.

Mia played soccer in college. Her team was called the Lady Tarheels. Mia helped the Lady Tarheels win all four years she played.

Mia jugaba fútbol en la universidad. Su equipo se llamaba *The Lady Tarheels*. Mia ayudó a su equipo a ganar durante los cuatro años que jugó en la universidad.

Mia also played on the United States Olympic Team in 1996. The Olympic Games were in Atlanta, Georgia, that year. Mia and her team won the gold medal.

Mia también jugó en el equipo olímpico de los Estados Unidos en 1996. Aquel año los Juegos Olímpicos tuvieron lugar en Atlanta, Georgia. Mia y su equipo ganaron la medalla de oro.

13

On May 22, 1999,
Mia scored her 108th
international goal.
International means
with other countries.
This was a record.

El 22 de mayo de
1999, Mia anotó su gol
internacional número
108. Internacional
significa que tiene que
ver con otros países.
¡Esto fue un récord!

Lots of people love Mia.
She is a great soccer
player and a great person.
Her fans let her know how
much they love her.

———————

Mucha gente admira a
Mia. Es una gran
jugadora y una magnífica
persona. Sus seguidores
siempre le demuestran
su afecto.

By Morgan Robinson #1 fan

17

Many of Mia's fans ask for her autograph. They want to remember meeting Mia forever.

Muchos de sus admiradores le piden su autógrafo. Quieren recordarla por siempre.

In 1999, Mia played for the United States in the Women's World Cup. Mia and her teammates won the World Cup. This made them the best women's soccer team in the world.

En 1999, Mia jugó con la selección de los Estados Unidos en el Campeonato Mundial de Fútbol. Mia y sus compañeras de equipo ganaron la copa y se convirtieron en el mejor equipo femenino de soccer del mundo.

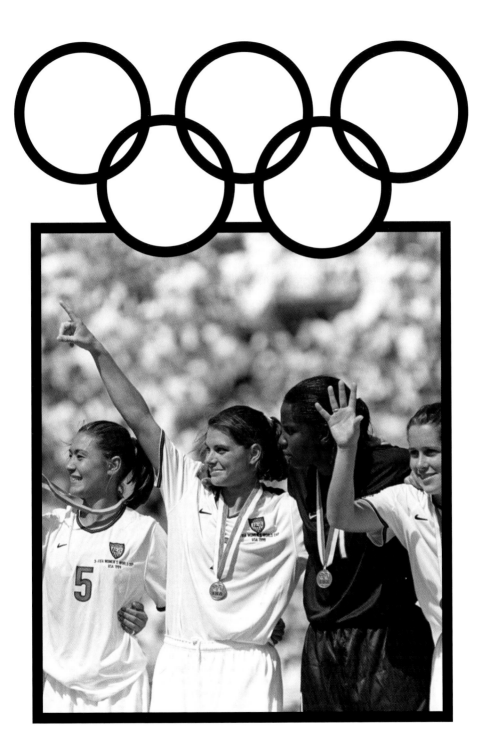

Glossary

goal (GOHL) When you put the ball in the other team's net. In soccer your team gets one point for a goal.

Olympic Games (oh-LIM-pik GAYMZ) A world sports competition.

record (REK-urd) When a player or team does something better than any other player or team ever has.

scores (SKORZ) When a player gets a point for a team.

soccer (SOHK-er) A sport where two teams kick and pass the ball without using their hands. Each team tries to get the ball into the other team's net.

Women's World Cup (WUH-munz WURLD KUP) A soccer competition, played by women every four years, to decide which team is the best in the world.

Glosario

Campeonato Mundial de Fútbol Femenil Torneo de fútbol soccer que se juega cada cuatro años.

gol Cuando metes el balón en la portería del otro equipo. Tu equipo gana un punto por cada gol.

Juegos Olímpicos (los) Competición deportiva internacional que se realiza cada cuatro años.

récord Cuando una persona o equipo hace algo que supera lo que han hecho otras personas o equipos.

soccer, fútbol Juego entre dos equipos en el que los jugadores impulsan un balón con los pies para pasarlo por la portería contraria.

Here is another good book to read about Mia Hamm:

Para leer más acerca de Mia Hamm, te recomendamos este libro:

Mia Hamm: Good as Gold
by Mark Stewart. Children's Press

To learn more about soccer, check out these Web sites:

Para aprender más sobre fútbol soccer, visita estas páginas de Internet:
http://wwc99.fifa.com
http://www.womensoccer.com

Index

Índice